Celestial Unification

Project

Remembering Who We Are

by

Mary Jane Adams

cover art by Christine Kesara Dennett

Avid Readers Publishing Group

Lakewood, California

Celestial Unification Project

Remembering Who We Are

All Rights Reserved

Avid Readers Publishing Group

http://www.avidreaderspg.com

ISBN-13: 978-1-935105-08-4

Printed in the United States

Acknowledgments

To Joseph, Linda and Donna for their
unwavering support
during my unconventional phases, especially
in the early years,
and to Lauren and Matthew for teaching me how
to be a child again.

Dedication

To My Beloved Friend and the celestial chorus
of angelic beings guiding humanity in
remembering the sacredness and unity of all
creation.

Contents

Introduction

Welcome, as you remember, realize and renew your dedication to bring joyful coexistence to planet Earth. You may not consciously recall your commitment to this Divine Plan, but your soul does. It is nudging you forward to become fully aware of the magnificence of the human race and its ability to bring peace on earth and good will toward all humankind. The angelic realms proclaimed this great undertaking in millennia past. I now refer to that prolific announcement as the Celestial Unification Project or simply CUP.

Spiritual memories lying dormant since time immemorial are being awakened as we, the participants in this project, are experiencing a quickening to fully comprehend the

awesome beauty of a mission so monumental it will bring about the changes in the world we are actively seeking.

This book emphasizes my memory of CUP. I often describe the process as my spiritual elementary school education in learning the 3 R's --- Remembering, Realizing, Renewing. By the time you finish reading these stories, my hope is you also will remember, realize, and renew your membership in the Celestial Unification Project.

Is there a pulsating rhythm behind the physical heartbeat? Is there a sublime knowing behind the conscious mind? Is there an ineffable essence to human nature waiting to be rediscovered? What is the purpose of life? Who am I?

Since an early age, those profound questions percolated in the recesses of my mind. Searching for answers started me on a journey learning to embrace the mystical moments of not only my life but all creation.

This is a spiritual memoir, but not exclusively mine. It is ours. It is not an intellectual pursuit but a flowing from one open heart to another. It is the vibration of individual souls recognizing the unity of all souls written in the language of love.

How do I explain the subjective, thought provoking and believe it or not scenarios that have transpired to anyone not familiar with my life or me? How can I publish such intimate details? If a friend spoke to me about what I have written, I would think, "What an imagination she has!" But, I would listen objectively and make my own decision. That is what I am asking of you. See beyond the printed word. Feel the pangs of your heart. Hear the whispers of your soul.

Every episode I describe has been personally experienced. For many years I have kept a diary which has played an

integral part in these writings. In order to recall dates of particular events, it was necessary to reread the entries. That exercise proved to be a wondrous undertaking. As I relived specific incidents, their beauty and inspiration continued to fill me with awe. Even as I type these words, my heart swells with gratitude for the ability to share them.

You will discover this is not a how-to or step-by-step book promising enlightenment. However, if someone wanted to label this a Self-help book with a capital S, I would agree. You and I are the capital S. You and I are the Self in the Self-help. A chapter entitled, "The Seven Keys" is the closest how-to section. The Keys outline ways to enhance a positive lifestyle. They were presented in remarkable, yet ordinary, sets of synchronistic situations.

The events mentioned throughout this volume are sprinkled with poetic rhymes revealing my inward

journey although my intention is for these experiences to provide nourishment for you to seek or continue your own journey. A journey knowing, not just believing, that the spark of divinity is within every human being allowing each of us to say, beyond a doubt, that we are one with the Universal Creative Spirit which we collectively call God residing within ourselves and all creation. I believe our mission in life is to remember this oneness. It is the quest for the Beloved, our true Divine Friend. We are the vessel, or CUP, for the Divine to express.

I do not recall a specific moment or circumstance that lead me to take the proverbial first step, but I do remember making God a priority in my life. The strong dedication of wanting to know about God resulted in the stories contained in these chapters and what has been presented as the Celestial Unification Project.

After wholeheartedly pledging myself to the spiritual

path, I became aware of a previously veiled presence which I call My Beloved Friend. Each human being is gifted with this Friend, a Friend who reminds me of a silent, yet persistent passenger, in an exquisite vehicle. We steer this vehicle (our body) on a spiritual highway, intuitively guided by the navigation system of the Soul, fueled by Divine grace.

Eventually, the perseverance with which we begin the journey turns to devotion. This devotion tends to lessen the inevitable potholes, twists, and turns along the way. At times the storms of life make the road slippery. We may skid into a ditch, practically buried in mud, but it is then that we learn the strength of our spiritual muscles to pick ourselves up, get back in the driver's seat and once again move toward our destination of remembering who we are and our unity with all.

When I started this amazing trip, assurances from friends,

business associates, community leaders and individuals in religious communities were essential to my knowing that men in white coats were not waiting to put me in a straightjacket. Those dear ones convinced me I was normal, living a contemporary existence in modern society, albeit some with a twinkle in their eye and a smile on their face.

My parents were members of the Catholic Church. Subsequently, I attended both grammar and high schools affiliated with that denomination. However, a deeper understanding and knowing of who or what God is, eluded me.

As a young adult, I began studying various sacred traditions. Those studies demonstrated that the core teachings of the world's major religious institutions, when stripped of dogmas and creeds, were essentially the same.

The mystical elements of the orthodox religions intrigued me the most. In Judaism it was the cabbala; in Christianity the contemplative lives of saints such as Teresa of Avila and John of the Cross; in Islam it was the Sufi tradition and in Buddhism and Hinduism it was the emphasis on meditation.

An eclectic group of people, exploring similar interests, entered my life during this time of self-discovery. New friendships developed that became an intricate part of my seeking. Teachers appeared and inspirational literature fell off bookstore shelves. Devouring the lives of ancient and modern saints, mystics and philosophers, propelled me forward. What did they know? How did they find it? If there was secret knowledge, what was it? I was committed to understand, as best I could, what God is or isn't and what I am or am not.

Many years passed. Meditation became an essential part of my daily routine. Then, without any fanfare or trumpets blaring, an innate knowingness surfaced --- "the Kingdom of God is within." Wait a minute! That's not new information. I heard that as a child. But, something switched in my perception.

The personal everyday experiences revealed in this volume took me to a place of knowing, not just believing, that "the Kingdom of God is within." Then the answers to those original philosophical questions became easier to comprehend and seemingly made the unknowable somewhat more knowable.

Family and friends encouraged me to compile these writings although my resistance was high. Years went by as I procrastinated. Finally, I finished the manuscript but knew the project was not complete. As spiritual insights revealed themselves, it seemed I had just scratched the

surface. Each experience humbled me to the vastness of what loomed ahead. There was so much more to explore, so much more to learn. Yet, how could I not share with my entire human family the timeless and eternal truths of faith, hope and love already unveiled? Hence, the publication of this book.

Relive with me the adventures of this sacred story so you will recognize your own. Be aware of the energies surging from your soul as you remember your role as co-creators in the Celestial Unification Project traveling with an angelic Presence, your own Beloved Friend. Keep an open mind. Enjoy the ride knowing each word is true, believe it or not.

Mary Jane Adams

Chapter 1

The Golden Essence

It was a dream like no other, or was it? The date is July 7, 1989. Nothing is out of the ordinary. I go to bed at 11:00 o'clock that night. Suddenly my body jerks and a floating sensation has me suspended over a breathtakingly beautiful beach. With my senses heightened, I see iridescent turquoise water and feel it caress my feet as it gently laps against the golden white seashore. Each grain of sand and drop of water are effervescent with a light that defies description. "Where am I and how did I get here?"

The powder-like sand is neither wet nor dry. The cloudless

sky is the bluest blue imaginable. To the left is a cliff covered with dense foliage of the deepest green, vibrantly alive like the sea. The cliff extends into the ocean forming a perfect crescent bay. Coming around the bend of the bay is a gliding golden light that rests upon the beach.

Transfixed by this brilliant golden light, I see it is not a light but a living being. Every characteristic of this being is of a sun-lit hue. The form is clothed in a flowing loosely belted robe. The hair is shoulder length. Facial features are unrecognizable. The light surrounding the face is too intense. There is a feeling of immeasurable tranquility as a very tall golden figure approaches.

Even though the image appears to be a man, it is androgynous, neither male nor female. (For simplicity purposes only, the masculine pronoun will be used throughout this book.) There is a pure nurturing essence of love and peace emanating from this brightness. I have

no fear.

As he comes closer, his arms open wide and I literally walk into this golden presence. Every cell and atom of my body can be felt merging with this essence. A profound peace prevails as I am encased in golden radiance.

It is at this point that remembering details cease. I am fully conscious and aware of a knowingness but have no idea what the knowingness is. Nonverbal dialog is taking place. There is a voice, yet there is not a voice. I ask the question, "How am I going to remember all of this?" The response was, *"You will remember when you are suppose to."*

At that precise moment, I realized the experience must end. I pleaded for that not to happen. I did not know if I was dead or alive. If I was dead, it was okay. If I was alive, it was okay. Nothing seemed to matter except the total

peace and immeasurable love I was feeling. Then in the same nonverbal communication, I was told emphatically, yet with gentle compassion, that I must return to my life.

I begged to remain, but to no avail. Reluctantly I surrendered to the inevitable. The authority of this golden presence was unmistakable. Without a moment's hesitation, an energetic feeling of separation took place. Nevertheless I pleaded once more, "If I must go, please please let me remember, let me remember."

Instantaneously, I am standing next to this luminous figure and somehow had the wherewithal to ask, "Who are you?" He answers in the sweetest flawlessly toned voice, *"I am your teacher."* At that precise moment, my body jerks and I am lying in bed fully awake and thinking, "I remember. I remember. Thank you, thank you, thank you. I remember." Then, a slight pressure descends on me like a warm blanket of tender peace. I repeat, "Thank you for

letting me remember."

For an undetermined amount of time, I laid motionless in bed. Seeing my husband sleeping and the familiar surroundings of our bedroom assured me I hadn't left this life. I looked at the clock. It was shortly after 4:00 A.M. on July 8, 1989.

To say I love all forms of music is an understatement. Certain songs touch me deeply. The lyrics and melodies soothe me as I navigate through my day. In fact, most every room in our home has a radio or CD player in it.

When I awaken each morning, the first thing I do is turn the radio on. That particular day was no exception although the hour was extremely early. However, there was something different about the energy of the room. I could not pinpoint it.

Then, from the radio, I heard the first few notes being broadcast. The song was "Beyond the Sea" sung by Bobby Darin. The lyrics have a mystical quality referring to transcendent locations filled with sublime metaphors. My heart pounded rapidly as I listened to phrases such as "golden sands" and "beyond the stars".

I felt an electric current run through my body as those words emanated from the radio. They were strikingly similar to how I best describe the dream I just had. That song validated the experience of walking on golden sands with a golden essence. I felt energized, exhilarated, and wanted to experience more. I was not disappointed.

When my husband Joseph woke up, I told him about the dream and hearing "Beyond the Sea". I also explained that something felt different. Everything was still the same, but not quite, and I did not even know what that meant. He just smiled and said, "You have to start writing

this stuff down. There's something going on here."

That dream, nearly 20 years ago, was not the first time an unusual incident happened. Joseph always encouraged me to write about them. As a result of his nudging and the extensive notebooks that followed, this book could not have been written. Joseph continues to support my spiritual endeavors although he does not actively pursue them himself. He has been my witness on several occasions confirming these remarkable and curious events.

The synchronicities of that day continued to unfold. While driving to an early morning exercise class, a different version of "Beyond the Sea" sung by George Benson was on the car radio. The same song again! It was not popular in 1989. To hear it twice within the span of a few hours was highly unlikely. In fact, it had been nearly 30 years since the record was a hit in 1960. Was someone or something trying to get my attention? If so, it

was working. I felt like Alice in Wonderland with things getting curiouser and curiouser.

The icing on the cake came later that afternoon upon arriving home. As my car entered the driveway, an instrumental version of "Beyond the Sea" performed by pianist Roger Williams echoed in my ears…three different radio stations, three different versions of the same song. All heard within hours of having "dreamt" of a beautiful sequence of events taking place beyond the sea with a golden essence on a golden beach. It was a coincidence like no other, or was it?

My Beloved Friend, *let the words flow*
Allowing me to glow
In the presence of you
Times majestic view.

Golden arms unfold
The story is told
It's one of peace
Or my world will cease.

My Beloved Friend, journey with me
Beyond the sea
A golden beach
Is where I teach
A gentle song
Not very long
Filled with peace
Never to cease.

Chapter 2

An Ordinary Person

Although this book is not an autobiography, I believe sharing some personal information is appropriate to gain perspective into my background. I was born August 27, 1943 in Waukesha, Wisconsin, the eldest of five children. My early upbringing would be considered typical of small town America in the mid-20th century.

My father immigrated to the United States from Yugoslavia with his parents in the early 1920's. He was a blue-collar worker devoted to his family. We were neither rich nor poor --- no country club membership but we were one of the first families on the block to have a television set.

Strong values of respect for community and family were instilled at an early age.

Mother was a homemaker during my early childhood. She is of Polish descent from Milwaukee, Wisconsin who was also raised by immigrant parents. She continues to be involved in my life. One of the earliest memories of my mother was her love of music. I remember listening to songs sung by Peggy Lee, Frank Sinatra, the Andrew Sisters, Tony Bennett and Perry Como. It was her early influence that attracted me to a variety of music.

It had been my father's dream to live in California. He heard all the post World War II stories of employment opportunities available in the fledgling aerospace industry and decided California offered more than Wisconsin.

By 1956 my parents had four children. My sister Patty was 9 years old; my sister Kathy, 6 years of age; my

sister Debbie, six months and me, 12 years of age. We all crammed into a 1953 Buick and drove the famous Route 66 to our new home in Los Angeles. My brother, David, was born two years later.

On January 1, 1959, just two and one-half years after our move, my father died unexpectantly from a massive heart attack. It was a devastating time. Mother was only 36 years old with five children, the youngest not quite three months old. She decided the best thing for our fatherless family was to return to Wisconsin where her parents and siblings lived.

Destiny led me back to Southern California in 1961 after graduating from high school. I lived with an aunt and uncle in Santa Monica, worked at Hughes Aircraft Company as a secretary, and married my first husband in 1962. Our daughter, Linda, was born in January 1964 followed by the birth of our second daughter, Donna, in

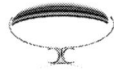

January 1965. Having two babies within one year kept me at home tending to their needs.

Both daughters have grown to be responsible adults, excelling in their chosen fields. They and my grandchildren, Lauren, born in October 1999, and Matthew, born in October 2002, are my greatest achievements.

Life took a detour in 1971 when my first marriage ended in divorce. I returned to the work force and two years later met Joseph. We were married in 1973.

Everyday events continued in a normal manner, whatever that means. Parenting, working, being with family and friends were important, but there was a stirring within pushing me to explore unknown territory. There was a questioning that somehow life was more than what appeared on the surface. More of what, I did not know, just something more.

When I began the quest of finding what that "more" was, a deep yearning developed, a yearning so strong that it accelerated my spiritual journey.

Now, nearly 40 years later, this book has been written to share my story with ordinary people like me, or are we? Maybe nothing is ordinary, just extraordinary.

My Beloved Friend, *a reflection of me*
For all to see
Within the eyes
There's no disguise.

Remember with me
It is the key
To all I give
For us to live.

My Beloved Friend, *open the book*
And take a look
It's easily read
To see ahead.

Silver wings take flight
Heading for the light
You're looking brand new
It's still up to you.

Chapter 3

My Beloved Friend

The poetic rhymes included at the end of these chapters were not authored by me. I am merely the scribe and cherish the source as My Beloved Friend.

Although it has been 17 years since July 17, 1991, I still respect the monumental request beckoning me that morning. At the time, my daily routine was to awaken at 4:30 a.m., have breakfast, read the newspaper and meditate before preparing to leave for work. The hours shortly after dawn were ripe for me to enter the silence. It was and still is the most peaceful part of my day.

After the children moved from our home, I redecorated and turned one of the bedrooms into a sanctuary where I could study metaphysical subjects and meditate. However, that particular morning offered no serenity. After considerable restlessness, a nonverbal voice said, *"Pick up a pen and write."* I thought, "What is this? Who are you? I don't want to pick up a pen and write. I want to sit here and meditate. I want to be quiet. I have a busy day ahead at the office. Writing is too much like work. Besides, what would I write?"

Trying to reenter the silence became a futile task. I was agitated and annoyed at the phrase that kept popping into my head, *"Pick up a pen and write."* It would not stop. It continued getting louder and louder as I tried getting quieter and quieter. Finally, there was no escape. I must do as told. The words were spoken in the same authoritative, yet compassionate style, as the voice from the "beyond the sea" dream. It was impossible to ignore. Surrendering

to an unknown presence was all I could do.

Finding a piece of paper and pen was easy. What to write was not. That thought had barely crossed my mind when three words seemed to flow from the pen unto the paper, *"My Beloved Friend."* Other eloquent, yet simple, words followed. To my amazement, they rhymed.

The subsequent poems each contained a descriptive story or thought process, usually just eight lines in length. Between July 17, 1991 and October 11, 1992, there were 129 *"My Beloved Friend"* rhymes. From October 11, 1992 until February 27, 1994, there were 46 *"My Beloved One"* poems. On May 17, 1994, the *"My Beloved"* verses began. There were times when other forms of poetry were presented and occasionally lengthy narratives.

The energy behind the *My Beloved Friend, My Beloved One* and *My Beloved* poems is the same with subtle

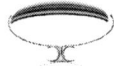

differences. I liken it to finding a genuine life partner, be it in marriage or friendship, male or female. First, there is the initial meeting and longing to be with that certain person, *My Beloved Friend*. Secondly, realizing this person is very special and the two of you are destined to be together, *My Beloved One*. Thirdly, there is an absolute knowing this someone represents a union with something greater, *My Beloved*, a divine friendship of sweet pure innocent unconditional love. The Greek word agape best describes the feeling.

The progression of the rhymes turned out to be a systematic process corresponding to a degree of understanding that I was acquiring on the spiritual journey. They continue to this day although the need to designate between *My Beloved Friend, My Beloved One* or *My Beloved* is no longer necessary.

I attribute the purpose of the different beginnings to be

an educational tool in realizing the oneness of life. The wondrous verses are likened to cobblestones on the path of remembering the relationship we share with our Creator and our participation in the Celestial Unification Project and its mission.

My Beloved Friend,
A knock on the door
To forevermore
Turn the key
And see it's me
A warm embrace
Seeing your face
Welcome again
Let us begin.

My Beloved One,
From the realms of light
Eternal love shines bright
It flows down through
All aspects of you
Reaching the heart
Signaling your part
In awakening man
To God's Great Plan.

My Beloved,
I am alive in the beingness of you.
The life of you is me
The breathe of you is me
The light of you is me
The love of you is me
I am alive because you are the beingness of me.

Chapter 4

A Cobblestone Path

There was a short two-block cobblestone street reminiscent of a bygone era in the small Midwestern town where I grew up. As a young girl, I remember envisioning antique automobiles bouncing along the uneven pavement.

As pleasant memories of a carefree childhood flooded my mind, that cobblestone roadway became a visual description of stepping-stones along the spiritual pathway. Each stone depicted a different teacher, book, essay, synchronistic event, conversation, rhyme, or dream that empowered my journey. When I was bumping through

life like the old cars on the rough pavement, disharmony was evident in my relationships with family, co-workers, and life in general. I didn't like the discontent. How could I feel evenness on the cobblestones?

Over the years I have learned that each person has unique cobblestones tailored to their own personality and lifestyle. My teachers are not someone else's or vice versa, although they can be the same. Recognizing a true cobblestone is at times difficult. Discernment is a necessary quality and occasionally trial and error proved to be my best teacher. Eventually, learning to trust my intuitive nature made the discernment easier. But it did not happen over night.

Patience was a virtue I truly needed while traversing the cobblestones. Ultimately, I found that the authenticity of the cobblestones was confirmed by the love, compassion and tolerance for the total well being of all persons involved.

Throughout the 1970's and 80's, I explored various world religions, some traditional, some not, and found the mystical elements most fascinating. They turned out to be true cobblestones. Much inspiration and appreciation for all belief systems resulted, but something escaped me. The road was still bumpy. What could make the ride smoother? What was the key element leveling the space between the cobblestones?

Meditation was emphasized at the many gatherings I attended. What exactly is meditation? Was it the link smoothing out the pavement? Was it the elusive element? I wanted to learn as much as possible. Soon meditation became a priority.

In today's society, there are many books, teachers and classes on the subject, but 30 years ago meditation had not as yet joined America's mainstream culture. I had to

dig deep into finding the right resources necessary to learn the discipline associated with it. In the early 1970's, a person practicing meditation was considered a bit kooky and living on the outskirts of society. In fact, members of my family wondered if I was being influenced by a cult.

In rather coincidental ways, this wanting to meditate brought forth not only instructors but also a vast array of literature, mainly from Buddhist and Hindu sources. I devoured everything I could read, attended seminars, workshops and lectures with influential speakers. It was an exhilarating time. I felt like a kid in a candy store. I hadn't realized it was just the tip of the iceberg.

After a chance meeting with a friend whom I had not seen in many years, more of the iceberg became visible. She introduced me to the teachings of Paramahansa Yogananda. Yogananda is considered by many to be a modern day saint. He was a holy man from India who

came to the United States in 1920 and founded Self-Realization Fellowship, a worldwide organization devoted to spiritual teachings. He passed from this world in 1952. The literary masterpiece, "Autobiography of a Yogi" was written by him. Reading it for the first time was transforming and brought clearer insight into meditation and living a spiritual life. I recommend it highly.

In the mid-1980's I started attending services at Self-Realization's Lake Shrine Temple in Pacific Palisades, California. Upon entering the small chapel for the first time, I saw beautiful portraits of the gurus (teachers) of Self-Realization. As I was about to take my seat, but still standing in the aisle, my knees got wobbly. I became disoriented and felt an impenetrable silence surround me as my eyes focused on a gentle serene image of Jesus.

It was a picture I thought I would never see in a Hindu temple. Front and center, next to Krishna and Yogananda

was the Great Master Teacher. Many years earlier I had run from what I thought were Jesus' teachings only to learn that I really didn't know exactly what he taught. I was instructed by what other people's interpretations were.

I had searched 20 years and found myself in a shrine based on Hinduism gazing at a picture of Jesus. It was a surreal experience. The portrait was not the Jesus of my early upbringing. I needed to find out more about this place and Paramahansa Yogananda. Perhaps the genuine Jesus, not a compromised version, could be found by studying the principles of self-realization as taught by Yogananda.

The importance of meditation was not new to me but never before had it made such an immense impact. Yogananda's ancient meditative techniques were paramount in my spiritual growth and fulfilled the legendary saying, "When the student is ready, the teacher appears."

As a result of devoting daily time to meditation, I discovered a peaceful knowingness of a love beyond life that worked through life. I call this love God and that this God is a God of good who loves unconditionally no matter what religious beliefs, or lack of them, human beings possess.

My definition of God may be different than yours. To me, God is the universal Essence of Love and Compassion, the benevolent Force of creation, not a grandfather figure sitting on a cloud. It is the Creator Spirit, ever present in and around all creation, whose loving embrace enfolds everything. It is a constant Energy reminding me we share the same Spirit.

Where did the erroneous thought of disconnection from this Creative Source come? Could the collective human race have, over eons of time, perpetuated the concept of

separation as a tool for survival? It's possible. But, all I do know is that being preoccupied with the duties and stresses of life caused me to put any resemblance of a divine connection "on hold". I knew something had to be done to remember the connection.

Meditation was my answer. It was the compelling influence in realizing a connection to God and an awareness of the Celestial Unification Project. It brought forth remembrances of the unity of creation and the Higher Self. This Higher Self, the Beloved Friend, became a true companion, not just a remote concept.

Tranquility surfaced as a result of the meditations and extended into every aspect of my life. Meditation's value cannot be highlighted enough. It truly is the elusive element holding the cobblestones together making the pavement on the spiritual path smoother.

When focusing on the loving and compassionate energy that meditation conveys, life is calmer. There is an ability to handle whatever presents itself in a more relaxed atmosphere. The experience of living in the "now" moment is intensified. Meditation is the method that has allowed me to feel and remember the very palpable energy of God that I call the Holy Spirit.

My Beloved Friend, *there is a place*
No time or space
Entered by you
And others too
Who let love pour
Through the door
Into the cup
That's opened up
The world again
Let peace begin.

My Beloved Friend, *love is the spark*
Living in the heart
Dispelling the dark
We're never apart.

Listen to hear
So gentle and near
The voice for you
That is the cue.

Chapter 5

The Emerging Earth

A significant dream took place the night of July 5, 1987. I am with a companion but unable to give him or her a name. We are looking down at the planet Earth from a high vantage point. There are twinkling stars all around. The view is spectacular, but something is terribly wrong.

Great sorrow overcomes me. The Earth does not look like the familiar photographs taken by the astronauts. The North Pole region can be seen peaking out of a brown crust that surrounds the planet. There is no visible blue marble-like effect of oceans, the outline of continents or

cloud cover, only a thick haze looking similar to a brown eggshell encasing the Earth. The sight was so disturbing I had to look away.

My fellow traveler knew my sadness and tenderly said, *"Look again, Mary. We did it."* As I turned around, a new scene appeared. It overwhelmed me. Our jeweled blue and white planet glistened as it rose up through the brown crust. A luminous rainbow of immense power was pushing the Earth into a radiant pulsating whiteness that seemed to contain every color in the spectrum but still remained brilliantly white.

The dream vanished as soon as I saw this Emerging Earth. Instantaneously, the lamp on my nightstand lit up. I am awake. Who turned the light on? I remember the dream. My husband is sleeping next to me. There is no one else in the room or in our home. I do not know how the lamp "turned itself on." It is another unexplainable situation

but nonetheless true.

When a dream like that occurs or a lamp automatically turns on, I do not broadcast such events to family or friends unless confirmation in "real life" takes place. In fact, one of the purposes in sharing these dreams and stories is to illustrate how validations come about in everyday life from unexplainable experiences. It took a mere three days for evidence of the Emerging Earth dream to manifest.

Friends invited me to attend the Church of Daily Living in Costa Mesa, California. I had not heard of the church before but they thought a group meditation service and lecture about the upcoming Harmonic Convergence of August 16th and 17th would interest me.

Upon entering the outer lobby of the church, the cover of a magazine jumped out at me. The Earth, surrounded by twinkling stars, was being pushed out of a brownish

colored eggshell by a glorious rainbow into shining white light. Just like my dream! I was excited and immediately told my friends of the dream. They too felt the exhilaration of the synchronicity as they looked at the vivid image.

In 1987 I had not seen the Earth represented in that manner, however, since then there have been numerous renderings with a similar theme. When trying to explain the imagery of the dream, I use the mythical Phoenix bird rising from the ashes. The Earth and all its inhabitants are ascending into an unknown greatness. It is a vision of newness creating hope for our planet with its present-day environmental and doomsday scenarios.

"Look again, Mary. We did it." Those precise words, expressed by my dream companion as we looked at the Earth, have given me hope not only for the preservation of our planet but also for the human race as the Celestial Unification Project unfolds. I feel a re-birth taking place

with the spasms of labor having already begun.

I believe it is up to each of us to take positive steps and commit ourselves to insuring the outcome of a brand new earth. We start small with our families, then branch out to friends, communities, and eventually this renewed spirit of cooperation will be felt around the world. Some people may say this is Pollyanna but I refuse to accept that. I had the dream and know it will happen. As the human race realizes its status as co-creators, empowered by the grace of the Creator, a purified world will rise from the ashes of our own burned out misconceptions of who we are.

A huge shift is occurring. Books are being written and speakers are expounding on these very themes, even the media has picked up the clarion call. The bandwagon of change is rolling. The message is being given and received in a myriad of ways, some scientific, some political, some spiritual. Nonetheless it is a recognized

fact that something needs to change and is changing. All involved are members of the CUProject whether they are aware of it or not.

This book is just one of the means bringing about a shift in consciousness whereby humanity has the opportunity to make the moral choice of preserving the planet and ourselves. That visionary dream of more than 20 years ago is manifesting. It continues to be a reminder of the hopefulness in the process of both our evolving planet and the human race, just as my dream escort said, *"Look, we did it."*

I have no doubt and am grateful to have been allowed to see the beautiful radiant Earth being cradled in the embrace of love inhabited by peaceful beings. We are those beings.

My Beloved Friend, *rainbows of light*
Brighten the night
Your voice I hear
So very near
The earth sails away
Bringing a new day
Of iridescent light
It's quite a sight.

My Beloved Friend, *showing all men*
The power's within
To lift the earth
For its new birth
Into a realm
You at the helm
Guiding with peace
Love's been released.

Chapter 6

Misplaced Wings

The Celestial Unification Project is not about a chosen few but all humanity. I believe we are celestial beings who have temporarily misplaced our wings. A beautiful dream illustrates those wings.

It is the night of December 8, 1992. I am in a state of deep sleep when a tremendous force propels me upward. I see an angelic form above me dressed in a garment of shimmering white. The delicate face was unrecognizable. Around what would be a waistline is a silvery belt with a huge light-infused blue crystal on it. A powerful magnetic energy was emanating from the crystal. I felt myself being

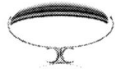

pulled up and out of my body. As this intense energy was lifting me up, there was no fear. I remember trying to figure out what was happening and who is with me.

The next thing I recall is my attempt to fly alongside this magnificent being when he says to me, *"You forgot how to use your wings. You need some lessons."*

He takes me to a structure resembling a large exquisite castle with round towers. As we seemingly fly through open windows into one of the towers, I notice the walls are encrusted with jewels of every conceivable color. I'm curious as to where I am and fascinated with the jewels. They look to be the size of large framed oil paintings. When I try to maneuver inside the tower, which now seems extremely small, I feel as though I'm about to somersault, head over heels. When my "flight instructor" sees me wobbling, he says with a chuckle, *"Remember you have wings and only tilt your head down when you*

are landing!"

When I heard the wording "landing," I find myself resting on a manicured deeply colored green grassy hillside with the castle behind me. The cloudless blue sky is sparkling overhead. There is no one around. Peace penetrates the landscape. I feel relaxed but have the thought, "What happened to my wings?" Instantly, my body jerked. My husband is shaking me awake. He said my body had been rolling frantically and he wanted to make sure I was okay. I told him I just had one of those remarkable dreams and was being taught how to fly!

The lesson I received from that dream is that it is now time to reclaim those celestial wings. In so doing, we realize every person on Earth will someday remember to claim their wings, even those we consider to be enemies. They too are responding to their lessons. We can honor their intrinsic angelic presence without condoning or judging

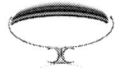

their actions. There is no timeframe within eternity.

> **My Beloved Friend**, *suspended above*
> *A magnet of love*
> *This crystal jewel*
> *Is the fuel*
> *Created by you*
> *To make things new*
> *Taught by the being*
> *You are seeing*
> *It's one and the same*
> *Whatever the name.*

> **My Beloved Friend**, *all answers are found*
> *Where love does abound*
> *To the lessons of life*
> *That cut like a knife.*

> *You need only to ask*
> *Then turn over the task*
> *To the teacher of all*
> *Who've answered the call.*

Chapter 7

Transcendent Dictations

During an early morning meditation on June 12, 1989 the words, *"I don't belong anywhere, I belong everywhere,"* exploded in my mind. I knew I did not consciously think them. Their transcendence was undeniable and beyond my intellect. So where did they originate?

All I know is that the previous night my prayer was for inspiration on how to handle a conflict. I was confused and fearful about an appointment scheduled the next day. When I heard, *"I don't belong anywhere, I belong everywhere,"* I knew the prayer was answered. It was the

perfect response to a question that would be asked of me. All apprehension concerning the outcome was gone.

There was no negativity or hurtful accusations during the meeting. An amicable outcome resulted which I attribute to the confidence instilled in me by those uncomplicated yet strong words. A heavenly source solved an earthly problem.

The gifted sentence, *"I don't belong anywhere, I belong everywhere,"* was given near the beginning of what I have labeled transcendent dictations. Dictation played an important role in my business career and, as it has turned out, in my spiritual quest.

Shorthand was a skill I performed daily as the personal assistant to the chairman of a multibillion-dollar corporation. In the 21st century, shorthand is practically a lost art. The technology of computers, text messages,

the Internet, cell phones and easy access to e-mail has practically eliminated its usage. In fact, when speaking to young people, they are puzzled as to what shorthand is. When I demonstrate it, they become fascinated with the sweeping curves of the symbols. Recently a young man saw me "scribbling" and asked if it was some sort of alien writing!

The transcendent dictations, including the *"My Beloved Friend"* rhymes, are plainly worded yet multi-layered in their interpretations. When I read the same phrase or sentence on different occasions, they somehow fit perfectly into what is happening at the moment. *"I don't belong anywhere, I belong everywhere,"* is a prime example. It helped my predicament at the meeting which, incidentally, occurred with a high-ranking person affiliated with a religious institution.

Ironically, I was studying a myriad of religious teachings

at the time and saw a connection with that sentence and religion. Among modern religious groups, there appears to be a "my way is the only way" mentality. It did not make sense to me in 1989 nor does it now. The Golden Rule of, *"Do unto others as you would have them do unto you,"* seems to be lost in creeds and dogmas. Then, when I hear a transcendent source say, *"I don't belong anywhere, I belong everywhere,"* my faith in a true religion based on love is restored.

How can religion be anything but a conduit to living the Golden Rule? How can an all-inclusive benevolence be enclosed in one particular building, shrine, temple, or sacred site when the major attribute of a munificent spirit is omnipresence? Where is the rationale for this Spirit to be contained and meant for only a specific group of people when we all belong to the human family? It would seem that, *"I don't belong anywhere, I belong everywhere,"* is a statement signally just such an omnipresence.

It is not my intention for you to take my word for anything I have stated or written. Listen to your heart and let your intuition reveal the answer. When you repeat, *"I don't belong anywhere, I belong everywhere,"* what does that mean to you? Trust your own transcendental persona to answer.

My Beloved Friend, *you went away*
One long ago day
But here I stay
On love's bright ray.

We did it together
Through stormy weather
Now clouds shine bright
With beaming light.

We remain steady
For those who are ready
The dawn is here
No need to fear.

My Beloved,
In the joy of creation
Your Light is My Light
Your Love is My Love
Your Peace is My Peace
Your Breathe is My Breathe
In the joy of creation you are,
My Beloved.

Chapter 8

The Still Small Voice
Speaks Loudly

While engulfed in a fast-paced corporate world, my home life frequently played second fiddle. Juggling a career, family, social activities, friendships and pursuing esoteric subjects was a 24/7 job. Life was simultaneously exhilarating, exhausting and exciting. However, during the mid-1990's, a simmering burnt out feeling consumed me.

Wanderlust surfaced and thoughts of taking a sabbatical took precedent over everything else. Traveling and being with people who shared my spiritual and meditative

practices intrigued me. The Hawaiian island of Kauai and Mount Shasta in Northern California were appealing locales to wallow away hours in solitude. Separating myself from a rigorous schedule was tempting.

Should I run off? What would happen if I did? Would I loose my job? Would my husband leave me? Would my children think I really was as crazy as they thought?

There was much to be considered. If I left, it would mean saying goodbye to a comfortable lifestyle. Supportive people surrounded me. They knew the importance of my spiritual path but how much could they endure? I knew they would not stand in my way but also knew my leaving would be disruptive to their lives. The unknown outcome was unsettling. Nevertheless, it was a captivating prospect that weighed heavily on my mind.

When I first approached the subject with my husband and

employer, there seemed to be no obvious resistance to my self-imposed exile. I thought, "This must be God's will. There are no obstacles. Everything is going smoothly. The universe is saying yes to my plan." I had forgotten the wise adage, "Man plans, God smiles." Then something outside the ordinary happened; another serendipitous dream.

It was September 28, 1996. I am exiting out of a clear crystal-like door that has no top, bottom or sides. The door appeared endless and yet it "opened." The same absolute blue cloudless sky, like the other dreams, engulfs me. The surreal environment was otherworldly. My thought is, "I need to see where I have been."

As I turn around, there is a large red heart etched on the front of the "door." Above the heart were bold black letters spelling out, "To God." As soon as I read those words, the familiar bodily jerk sensation occurred and I woke up in

bed remembering the dream. What just happened? Did I return from a heavenly encounter? I need to write in my journal. Perhaps its significance would become clear in the not too distant future. I didn't have to wait long. The future arrived the next morning.

The day's to-do list was full of shopping, picking up dry cleaning and other mundane duties. One of my stops was to purchase a CD at a local record store. As I left the store, I realized the door was clear-glass, very similar to the one in last night's dream. The only difference being no red heart, but there were bold black letters identifying the store. At the precise moment of realizing the doors were almost identical, an odd yet recognizable feeling overtook me. Time stood still.

There I was standing on the sidewalk, people walking, cars passing, life bustling all around and yet I was encased in a bubble of perfect silent stillness. Everyone seemed

oblivious to my situation.

The next thing I knew a familiar nonverbal voice said, *"It's not where you think you should be, it's where you find yourself, that's where it is."* Instantaneously, whatever was taking place was over. The noise in the parking lot returned. Where did the silence go? What just happened?

So as not to forget, I kept repeating, *"It's not where you think you should be, it's where you find yourself, that's where it is,"* until I was able to find a piece of paper and a pen. When I saw the words written, the idea of running off on a sabbatical was out of the question. I knew beyond a doubt that it was unnecessary to be anywhere except right where I was. Suddenly, Southern California seemed like heaven.

The still small voice spoke loudly that day. I have learned

to pay attention to its advice and stop trying to figure out where it came from or the source.

When I look at life as a witness and try not to dictate a certain outcome, something happens effortlessly and the situation vanishes into but a momentary distraction. *"It's not where you think you should be, it's where you find yourself, that's where it is,"* turned out to be a wonderful lesson in trusting the unknown and being in the present moment. Once again, heaven solved an earthly quandary. In the ensuing years, that phrase has helped me make many decisions.

My Beloved Friend, *a reflection of me*
For all to see
Within the eyes
There's no disguise
The voice you hear
Is so very near.

My Beloved Friend, *at the edge of a dream*
We are a team
Your voice whispers the word
And I have heard
Behold it is written
Now you must listen.

Chapter 9

Whoever Loves You Most,
I Love You More

Our family celebrates the Christmas season in joyous chaos. Decorations are abundant with more than enough food to savor for days. The festivities in 1993 were no different.

All the merriment and holiday revelry did not allow much time for meditation. In fact, I was feeling quite guilty for lacking the discipline to meditate. But, on Christmas day I wanted to at least say happy birthday, Jesus. Ten minutes was all I had before our daughters would arrive for the beginning of the traditional activities.

As I knelt before my altar, a sudden tenderness swept over me. A gentle soothing non-verbal voice whispered, *"Whoever loves you most, I love you more."* Tears welled in my eyes as strong emotions surfaced. I was overwhelmed with the sweetness of the moment. The self-inflicted guilt of not finding time to meditate vanished when those innocent words echoed the true meaning of Christmas.

That pure unconditioned sentiment of love cut to the core of the Christmas message. *"Whoever loves you most, I love you more,"* is a testament to the power of, "Peace on Earth, Good Will to Man."

It was that Christmas morning in 1993 when I realized no matter how active life gets, our soul essence is ever present. It only takes an awareness of the intimate dialog being conveyed to realize we are never alone. We are

like the Christ Child wrapped in swaddling clothes. We are being cuddled in a soft blanket of love by a devoted parent. *"Whoever loves you most, I love you more."*

When I have experienced feelings of such magnitude, it is easier to remember being a child of the Eternal Spirit. I may only have a short time to meditate, but do it anyway. It is in those moments, least expected, that the enormity of something greater emerges. God knows no time, only the heart whispering hello.

Typing "hello" reminds me of a visit to a gravely ill friend. It was a time for good-byes. As I entered the hospital room, a thought so incredibly preposterous and absurd crossed my mind. In fact, I almost left. An unseen voice told me to tell my dying friend to give Jesus a message. "That's ridiculous," I remember thinking, and felt foolish acknowledging such an outlandish request. I certainly did not have a clue to the nature of any message and felt

totally inadequate to convey anything to Jesus.

However, sensing this was a "beyond Mary" proposition and a lesson in trusting the still small voice and, more importantly, acting upon it, I relaxed, said a short prayer, and waited to see what happened. Almost immediately, my heart swelled with the words, "Say hello to Jesus from Mary."

A simple "hello" was the message. But I still felt foolish. Yet, it was a demand I couldn't ignore. I went to my friend's bedside and whispered those words.

She passed away shortly thereafter. It was sad for us gathered even though the nearness of life's final breath was expected. What wasn't expected was the peace permeating the room. It lingered for a considerable time. Those of us who remained spoke of a comforting presence filling our sorrow.

Wanting to hear some soothing music after leaving the hospital, I turned the car radio on. The melodic tune, *"Hello, My Friend, Hello"* was playing. My heart leaped as I felt an electric current flow through my body. While listening to those words, I definitely knew the message I whispered to my friend had been delivered and, *"Hello, My Friend, Hello,"* was the response.

You might ask, "How do I know with such certainty that was the case?" I don't. It cannot be proven, however, the heartfelt sincerity spoke beyond my need for proof of its authenticity. Oftentimes there is no explanation for such events…a coincidence perhaps? When a profoundly personal incident occurs that cannot possibly be known by anyone else, something amazing is taking place. My belief is that when such a private occurrence takes place, God talks. I cannot explain it. I have stopped trying.

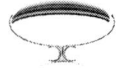

You may still consider this all a bit outlandish, and it's okay. I believe God is so personal that only through our most intimate thoughts and actions can we really know we are being spoken to. Our job is to find out how God speaks to us. Are we not all unique personalities leading diverse lives? Why wouldn't God whisper in a manner relevant only to the person receiving the message as it pertains to their personal life experience?

A loving monk at the Lake Shrine Temple of Self-Realization Fellowship would be telling an outlandish story relating to how God speaks in synchronistic, coincidental, and mysterious ways. When finished, he would conclude by saying, "believe it or not," giving his audience an impish grin as he left the podium. Although you are unable to see that grin, feel the awe of knowing certain things cannot be explained or proven, even though they are true. What a grand magnificent mystery of life!

My Beloved Friend, where's the gift
you say?
To give this Christmas Day.

Oh gentle one so wise
It's hidden in disguise
Within the soul of you
Left to unwrap and view.

It's given by Me
The One you cannot see
Smiling down on your face
Filling you with Grace.

My Beloved Friend, softly you speak
To those who seek
A gentle way
Throughout the day.

A Christmas dove
Wrapped in love
Brings the peace
For release.

Chapter 10

Celestial Unification Project

After being asked countless times to explain how the dictations, dreams, and rhymes come about, the best description is "inspired." The timing is unpredictable. I could be surrounded by nature, conversing with a neighbor, reading the newspaper, or listening to beautiful music when a slight energetic vibration or tingling (like goose bumps) signals me to write a word or two describing what just took place. Then, when circumstances permit, I generally sit in my meditation room and a dictation follows. At other times, it is not so simple.

As numerous notebooks were being filled with these

writings, my husband encouraged me to copyright the material. He also insisted that I acquire a "Doing Business As" legal document. Copyrighting was easy but obtaining the "d.b.a." meant coming up with a proper name, and that perplexed me.

While discussing an unrelated subject with a co-worker, the word "celestial" was mentioned. As "celestial" was verbalized, the tingling in my body reminded me that "celestial" needed to be written down, but being in a professional environment, the timing was not right. After returning to my desk, it still took several minutes before the opportunity to write "celestial" presented itself. Then the telephone rang. Business matters took precedent. "Celestial" had become just another word written on a message pad amongst a dozen other notes.

The next morning, while driving the Los Angeles freeway system not thinking of anything in particular, the words

"Celestial Unification Project" blazed across my mind with the familiar tingling sensation. Traffic was bumper to bumper. I could not stop to write that curious phrase down. So I continued to my destination.

As I drove into the parking structure of the building where my office was located, those strange words gripped me again. I had only a few minutes until a business meeting was to start. I needed to find a piece of paper quickly. A sense of urgency took over as I wrote "Celestial Unification Project" and the following was "dictated."

Celestial Unification Project (CUP) — the uniting, the blending, the coming together of God's beings of love remembering that each is doing a part uplifting the planet Earth and its inhabitants into the reality of constant communication with love, peace, joy and harmony universally in and through all creation bringing it into alignment with its celestial brothers and sisters.

CUP is the blending, the uniting of the Essence of Who We Are although we were never not blended or united. The CUP remembrance first takes place within individuals. Then the blending, the uniting, takes place within close relationships, then amongst all humans, then globally in all kingdoms, then galactically and then inter-galactically. It is upon completion of the blending, the uniting, that the Oneness of the Essence through all and in all celestial realms of Spirit is known.

Those two paragraphs flowed effortlessly. When finished, I hurriedly put the piece of paper into my purse and rushed into the building. I did not have time to read nor think about what was written.

It was much later in the day when I finally read the dictation. My emotions took over and tears formed. I knew immediately the name for the d.b.a.---*Celestial*

Unification Project---CUProject.

Once again a gift had been given during the routine of normal responsibilities. It dramatically showed me the inseparability of the spiritual and physical realms. It revealed the oneness of all and how spirituality is usually not found by being a hermit in a cave but in the practicality of living. We drive. We work. We love. We play.

A major lesson in the 3R curriculum of remembering, realizing and renewing is learning the delicate balance of spirituality and physicality. They are partners in the dance of life perfecting our ability to "be in the world but not of it."

Fifteen years have passed since the "Celestial Unification Project" was dictated. I have come to realize each human being is a member. The majority of people living in our war-torn world would tend to disagree with that last statement, but intuitively I have come to trust that a Divine Plan is working although I have no expertise in knowing how. Perhaps it is karma, or "what goes around, comes around," or "we sow what we reap." All I have is a trust in a Benevolent Intelligence radiating justice above the seeming negativity and knowing a greater Self gives comfort and support when needed to fulfill the Plan and overcome human flaws and worldly adversities.

My Beloved Friend, *a chalice of love*
Is filled from above
With crystal white light
That brightens the night.

Reaching the glory
Completes the story
It ends in peace
With a new lease.

My Beloved Friend, *time to wake up*
And see the cup
Brimming with love
Sent from above.

Bringing the peace
For all to teach
On planet earth
During rebirth.

Chapter 11

The Seven Keys

Attending Sunday morning church services was a pattern formed in childhood when attendance at Catholic Mass was mandatory. As an adult, I continued to worship in various churches and temples. The feeling of community and interaction with supportive people has always sustained me.

Services at the Agape Church in Los Angeles on Sunday, May 5, 1996, proved to be anything but routine. I arrived 45 minutes early to allow extra time for meditation.

Even with the best of intentions, meditation is not always easy, but that morning it was effortless. Quietness quickly transported me to an elegantly landscaped garden. I am standing on a pure white marble-like path which stretches endlessly before me. I see a flower covered arched trestle a short distance ahead. In the archway is a luminous figure clothed in white. His arms are stretched forward. He is holding seven large gold keys on his opened hands. He slowly walks toward me. I notice specific words on each key but can only read the inscriptions on two. I am confused and bewildered. I knew I had to remember the messages written. The "keeper of the keys" said; *"You will remember the others within 30 days."*

Upon hearing those words, I was jolted back out of the meditative state with the robust singing of the choir. The beautiful garden and glowing figure were still alive in my mind as I remembered the messages on the first two keys. I quickly fumbled for a pen and paper and wrote:

    1. Allow God in your life.

    2. Allow yourself to be YourSelf.

I attempted to listen to the remainder of the service as I pondered my vision and the messages on the seven keys.

Slowly but surely I was starting to trust the surprising incidents transpiring in my life and knew the remaining keys would be revealed, just not knowing how. I went about my typical schedule giving no conscious thought to the keys. Two mornings later, while putting on make-up, these words came, *"Allow others to be ThemSelves."* I knew it was key number 3. I was excited with the looming prospect of receiving the other keys.

Patience has never been one of my better virtues but I sensed a spiritual lesson or two in this latest episode. In waiting as long as 30 days, I was required to surrender my own agenda and trust the statement, *"You will know the others within 30 days."* I have discovered that surrendering and trusting are two of my primary lessons.

I distinctly remember driving to work when key number 4 came in a quick thought. Another time I was at the grocery store and there was key number 5. Key number 6 turned up while watching television and key number 7 while preparing dinner. All seven keys were disclosed within the 30 day timeframe, precisely as the angelic vision stated. They were exposed in diverse ways but in the most ordinary of circumstances. Life was being lived ordinarily and yet something extraordinary was happening.

Each key begins with the word "allow," a wonderfully compassionate and heartening word accentuating the positive side of life rather than the negative. They were received in the following order.

1. Allow God in your life.

2. Allow yourself to be YourSelf.

3. Allow others to be ThemSelves.

4. Allow the remembrances to come forth.

5. Allow trusting the unseen.

6. Allow forgiving yourself and others.

7. Allow the love of our Father to manifest.

Every time I read or recite the keys there is a powerful yet calming assurance of faith, hope and love in their straightforwardness. There is also recognition of deeper levels of understanding within the all-knowing words. I reflect upon them often and encourage you to do the same. Declare them out loud. Go within to meditate on their meaning especially for you and *allow* the still small voice to reveal the truth and wisdom contained in the simplicity of *allowing*.

I have intentionally not interpreted the keys in this book.

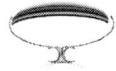

I strongly believe their meaning is to be perceived within the sacred space of your heart *allowing* the Beloved Friend to clarify the seven keys remembering, *"The Kingdom of God is Within."*

Chapter 12

A Velvet Brick

I have traveled many roads these past 35 years…some smooth, some bumpy. Through it all, meditation has been the map and the element smoothing the pavement allowing the intuitive voice to speak. Occasionally, I do not pay attention, usually for selfish reasons. Then unpleasant circumstances keep repeating until I once again unfold the map seeking clearer direction.

Life on our individual roadways seems to be accelerating at a phenomenal speed. This is just not my observation. The more I speak with others, they also agree. During these hurried times, we travel our highway without

viewing the scenery whizzing by. Instances to smell the roses, even a single rose, seem to have vanished. Everyday responsibilities engulf us and our spiritual life finds itself traveling on the back roads. Yet, I believe with all my heart, the discipline of meditation must be practiced.

I have said previously, and I'll repeat, balancing the spiritual and physical worlds is paramount to achieving our highest potential. That balance is attainable by creating a niche in our schedules to meditate.

After all these years, I still diligently find time to meditate and remind myself it doesn't have to be for long sessions or in so-called spiritual places. No matter the length, I ask that you join me and just do it. Make the effort and let God do the rest.

I recall hearing a story about Paramahansa Yogananda. He was asked, "Where is the best place to meditate? His

answer was, "In the middle of Manhattan."

Enlightenment is a word often used to explain the goal of meditation. I prefer to state the goal as remembering our connection with the Divine. When using the term enlightenment, I apply it as a metaphor to lightening up our lives…not being so burdened.

By conscientiously working toward attaining the Divine remembrance, we learn to accept our lives just as they are. We find fulfillment in relationships, careers, and religious beliefs. Eventually, living the principles of the *Seven Keys* becomes a reality. Just like breathing, you don't have to think about them. They become an active part of life and in the process troubles are lessened. The Beloved Friend has made them lighter.

This is a most exciting time. It feels as though the zenith of anticipated greatness is about to take place when humanity

actively lives in peace and harmony with all nature. This improved human family populates the envisioned, "Emerging Earth," and the words from that chapter, *"We did it,"* fill me with humble gratitude knowing we have been given such a majestic assignment to accomplish.

The CUProject, in its myriad forms, is contributing to the great awakening as we remember, realize and renew our balanced human and divine natures.

Our spiritual nature is the essence of the CUProject. It is the velvet brick causing a colossal impact sprinkled with the softness of grace. It showers us with life altering events and reassurances of peaceful coexistence knowing we are never abandoned or left to our own resources. The spark of divinity has never left. As Jesus stated, *"I am with you always."*

One of the foremost components of our mission in CUP

is to help our fellow man realize he too is an essential member, never alone or deserted. There is no bias allowed or brick unturned in the velvet embrace of love.

My Beloved Friend, *the heart played a song*
It wasn't very long
Awakening the crew
So honest and true.

A call from on high
It's time to say bye
The old is no more
You're through the door.

A new world to come
Time to beat the drum
Heard at the core
Of love's gentle roar.

My Beloved Friend, *the world does give*
A means to live
In time and space
To reflect your face.

Love fills all eyes
Seen by the wise
Touched by a hand
That leads the band.

As the song unfolds
It's out with the old
A new celestial tune
Sung by angels soon.

Chapter 13

We are Here for Others and Others are Here for Us

After leaving the corporate world in 2003, a plethora of possibilities spread before me. A blank canvas was ready to be painted. What would the first brushstroke be? What challenges would surface as the portrait of my new self took form? How could I best incorporate the lessons learned and enjoy life.

The delicate balance between the physical and spiritual realms seemed a logical start. It was time to incorporate the fruits of my labor. But it would still be a few years until the Celestial Unification Project would be actualized.

Being blessed with two grandchildren, I cherish spending time with them. The wonderment of their childhood continues to be a joy. Watching them explore nature for the first time and learn new skills has kept me young at heart. This interaction has complemented the core message of CUP...a message of hope, love and reverence for the continuation of all life.

This younger generation is ripe for the giant leap in human evolution. They seem to intuitively grasp values of the CUProject without the years of study most members of my generation have endured. Or perhaps we merely forgot the innocence of being children of God and became adults of God instead, thereby forgetting Jesus' decree to "become like little children."

In January 2005 conditions changed. The enjoy life scenario disintegrated as a doctor gave me a shocking

diagnosis. Cancer cells inhabited my uterus. How could that happen? My lifestyle didn't compute with the diagnosis. I never smoked, rarely drank alcohol, ate predominantly a healthy diet, and exercised. There must be a logical explanation other than a genetic predisposition. But according to my physician, there was not, although he agreed I did not fit the typical profile.

After the initial shock, I did what had become a natural pattern. When life was turned upside down and inside out, I sought solace and direction in meditation. My prayer was for peace and comfort not only for myself but also for my family. This health crisis presented another way of surrendering my will to a Greater Will. I needed to practice what I preached. Do I accept love or fear?

On January 30, 2004, Joseph and I were asleep and alone in our home. In the dream state that night, I "heard" Diana Ross sing loudly and clearly the lyrics to the song,

"Reach Out and Touch." We do not own any Diana Ross recordings or a version of that song. Her voice came from an unknown source. I woke up with the words running through my mind when an inner voice said, *"We are here for others and others are here for us."*

Another unquestionably authoritative sentence was conveyed. Those words expressed a dependence on collective cooperation. So heeding the advice, "to reach out and touch," and, *"We are here for others and others are here for us,"* I spent the following day telephoning friends letting them know my situation and asking for prayers.

Reaching out to others was uncomfortable for me and required a change in perception. My life had been structured to be the giver, not the receiver. Now it was imperative to relinquish that characteristic and accept the nurturing of others as a valuable lesson in allowing them

to express their affection.

The love and support of family and friends throughout my medical ordeal validated, *"We are here for others and others are here for us."* They were instrumental in my recovery as well as the medical profession. It demonstrated the power of the physical realm, but what about the spiritual?

Three days before my scheduled surgery, the heavenly energy of the Holy Spirit intervened by "reaching out and touching me" in a dream. It is so exceptionally personal that further explanation will be kept for another occasion. But once more, the combined efforts of the physical and spiritual accomplished a complete healing. The cancer diagnosis and subsequent clean bill of health confirmed the teachings I have meticulously pursued.

Having learned and relearned many lessons since placing

my metaphorical vehicle on life's bumpy highway, a predominate principle has prevailed. Taking action upon the messages revealed in the dreams, meditations, and written inspirations is a necessity. The mystical experience itself is not enough. Action allows the sacredness of seemingly mundane situations to shine forth in brilliant respect to a higher wisdom, a higher power, who is knocking on the door of our hearts to reveal Itself to itself. Be sure to open the door to reveal a new unlimited you.

You may or may not have visions or dreams. But you will be blessed with confirmations uniquely yours. You will notice little coincidences. You will be kinder. You will be more tolerant. You will be keenly aware of the good in life yet acutely sensitive to the injustices taking place and the sorrows reflected in faces around the world. You will see the tragedies, however, something is different. You will feel empowered to make a difference. You will know YourSelf to be a pivotal point in changing the course of

human history and planet Earth. You will know what Mahatma Gandhi meant when he said, "Be the change you want to see in the world."

I hope these stories have inspired and encouraged you to stay on the cobblestone path of your personal journey of self-discovery knowing all creation is one with the Divine Essence. It is the fundamental message of the Celestial Unification Project to remember, realize and renew our membership as co-creators of life witnessing the splendor of an emerging Earth.

As this book concludes, three simple thoughts come to mind: find time to meditate; be grateful for the precious moments spent with loved ones; live life in peaceful coexistence with all creation. In so doing, we are graced beyond measure for our efforts.

Eternal gratitude is expressed to My Beloved Friend in

helping me accomplish this monumental task and grateful
to you, dear reader, as a reflection of Your Beloved Friend.

*Enjoy life remembering we are here for others and others
are here for us.*

My Beloved Friend, *the flame of victory*
Rises up in glory
Signaling the start
Of a blazing heart
Called upon to unite
The world this night
Fulfilling the Plan
To say yes we can
And celebrate at last
A completed task.

My Beloved Friend, *blending the race*
Is taking place
Within the heart
No ones apart.

In a sudden flash
The door is unlatched
Revealing the new
Unlimited you.

Now conquer all doubt
You've traveled the route
No obstacles appear
Release the fear.

Give them to me
It's meant to be
The burden is mine
Rest in the Divine.

My Beloved Friend, *how do I thank thee*
Overlooking the sea
For the love you give
Each moment I live?

See me everywhere
In the quiet air
Rustling the trees
With a gentle breeze
On the silver wings
As the bird sings
In a human face
Like delicate lace
In the ocean wave
Is the Love I gave.

Mary Jane Adams
2390 Crenshaw Boulevard, #186
Torrance, CA 90501
Email: maryjadams@cuproject.com
Website: www.cuproject.com

Printed in the United States
122678LV00001B/205-216/P